AF400634

Gender Quake

Poems

by

Joelle Ruby Ryan

authorHOUSE™

1663 Liberty Drive, Suite 200
Bloomington, Indiana 47403
(800) 839-8640
www.AuthorHouse.com

First published by AuthorHouse 10/03/05

ISBN: 1-4208-6929-9 (sc)

Printed in the United States of America
Bloomington, Indiana

This book is printed on acid-free paper.

<u>Acknowledgements</u>

I have been lucky to have the support, care and love of many wonderful people over my thirty one years of life on this planet. The interest you have taken in my life and work has literally helped to sustain me. Some of your lives are included in these poems. I hope that I do justice to the profound impact you have had upon me. I wish to express the utmost gratitude for the positive energy you have given me over the years. I can not list all the people who have ever encouraged me or shown me kindness, but I wish I could. Please know that I notice your warmth and support and I appreciate it. I hope I can return even a fraction of the love that has been given to me by so many fabulous people.

By name, I wish to thank the following:

Isabella Dana Beaulieu, Stéfan Rafferty, James Ross, Jeanette K. Beal, Amy Vonderembse, Peter Welch, Amanda Monyak, Allison Ryan, John Ryan, Jason, Monica and Nieth Ryan, James and Nancy Ryan, Sarah Anne Thompson, Sam Costa, Lou Wolfe, Don Osgood, Dan Samson, Tony Paine, Kate Devlin, Melina Draper, David Crouse, Marlene Bomer, Diane Strong, Monica Chiu, Vicki Smith, Mary Moynihan, Catherine Adamsky, Kristine Baber, Jamie Stuart, Lisa Hartley, Fay and Errol Lam, Merissa Sherrill Lynn, Yvonne Cook-Riley, Jessica and Stacey, Kathleen Grace-Bishop, Mike Lavers, Jane Phillips, Paul Cody, Patricia Schwartz, Pauline Park, Cathy Kocarek, Jessie, Ben Caron, Rico, Chase Meedown, Logan Crawford, Matt Rice, Mel Klein, Courtney Anderson, Mariette Pathy Allen, Denise LeClair, Lata D'Mello, Mara Kiesling, Lisa Mottet, Samuel Lurie, Danielle Askini, Kathryn Castro, Kael Parker, Christina Gerken, Sile Singleton, Maria Kitsinis, Margaret Weinberger, Mim Easton, Carina Self, Gunner Scott, Chris and Holsen, Annette Lynch, Karen Mitchell, Paula Gilroy, and my Transgendered Mother, Janice Josephine Carney. Thank you to my deceased Grandmothers: Bessie Hardy and Madeline Ryan.

For their inspiration, thank you to:

Margaret Cho, Kate Bornstein, Leslie Feinberg, RuPaul, bell hooks, Barbara Smith, Minnie-Bruce Pratt, Wendy Carlos, Rachel Pollack, Alice Walker, Howard Zinn, Nelson Mandela, Roseanne Barr, Michael Moore, Maya Angelou, Dolores Kendrick, Susan Stryker, Spike Lee, Dean Spade, Imani Henry, Georgina Beyers, Kade Farlow, Eli Clare, Dred, Yosenio Lewis, Mauro Cabral, Cheryl Chase, Morgan Holmes, Maria Belen Correa, Diego Sanchez and Boy George.

Thank you to my pets, past and present. You never cared what gender I was and just showed me love: Casey, Daisy, Stormy, Pepe, Kayla, Yoda, Ilsa, Moshi, Je'bear, Albert, Chianti and Omar.

A huge thank you to the love of my life: Bailey Jaye Garvin—my partner, my friend and my trans brother. Thanks for being my best teacher and most persistent cheerleader. It is you more than anyone who has melted the sheets of ice around my heart. Thanks for showing me the myriad healing powers of undiluted and unconditional love.

Finally, to my GLBT sisters and brothers who are no longer here: thank you for your work to make the world a better place and the courage to live life as your truest self. We are all indebted to your brave and selfless actions. We remember:

Christine Jorgensen, Sylvia Rivera, Marsha P. Johnson, Sylvester, Divine, Alexander John Goodrum, Marcelle Cook-Daniels, Audre Lorde, Ukea Davis, Stephanie Thomas, Joseph Beam, Robert Eads, Paul Monette, Brandon Teena, Andrea Dworkin, Gwen Araujo, Harvey Milk, F.C. Martinez, Marlon Riggs, Essex Hemphill, Gloria Anzaldua, Debra Forte, Rita Hester, Pedro Zamora, Pat Parker, Venus Xtravaganza, Terrianne Summers, and all the rest whose very names are lost to history. You did not die in vain.

We Re-Member you and will carry on the torch of liberation and justice.

Contents

Acknowledgements v

Preface 1

I. Trial by Fire: Sissyhood Survivals

The First Poem 6

I am not a Poet 8

Some Entertaining Queens 11

Some Words About People.. 14

Inner Child 15

Hate 18

Boyhood Tears 19

For the Boy that I Was... 21

II. Casualties of Gender: Re-Membering Fallen S/heroes

Venus: Goddess of Love.. 24

The Rape of Brandon Teena.. 27

Unidentified Transvestite Male... 30

There is, Always 33

III. Warriors I Have Known

Dawn... 38

Morbidity 41

Two Trees 43

Slice.. 44

Junior High... 45

No More Sleepless Nights 48

IV. The Edges of Hope and Despair

Bus Ride.. 52

Iowa 54

Sex Change Dream 56

No More Courage 57

Layers 59

Alone Again 61

Psycho Tropics 64

I. A T-Girl's Dilemma 65

II. A T-Girl's Prayer 67

Snow Suicide 70

V. Standing (6'6") Tall: A TransAmazon's Empowerment

My Power Poem 72

I'm Doin' It My Way 75

Smiling 78

Campus Contradictions 80

Purpose 82

To Be Real 84

What's in a Name? 87

Do You Have a Wee-Wee? 90

VI. Just Say "No!" to Assimilation: Forwarding Radical Resistances

United We Stand 94

Do Not Pass 96

Why MTV Sucks 99

Porno Spam 101

A Poem to Gay Sell-Outs 104

Gender Suspects 107

G to the L to the B to the T 109

Fuck Your Binaries !!! 111

On the Dotted Line 114

VII. Love and Revolution

Feminism Lives 118

Sanctuary 121

Boi Lust 124

We Didn't Know a Lot of Things 126

Gender Quake 128

Afterword 130

Preface

The poems collected in this volume were written between the years 2000 and 2004. I have always been interested in writing, and recall writing poems in junior high school. One of these poems was called "The River" and was published in the local paper. I also wrote very long fictional stories, and remember having a writing conference with my seventh grade teacher about them. She pointed out that my protagonists were always female, and how that was remarkable. Most of the stories she saw had male students writing male protagonists and female students writing female lead characters. She saw my cross-gender writing as significant, and she was right-on! I knew by age five that I was "different," and by junior high I knew that though I was physically male, I did not identify with the masculine gender. Going through puberty and the teenage years is hard on anyone; for a kid struggling with their gender identity it is often a brutal nightmare. Some young people do not survive. At the time, I did not realize the importance of writing in my life. Looking back, I now see it as a life-saving activity. In a world where I was being verbally and physically besieged by my peers, I could always escape into the elaborate world of the written word. Through reading and writing, I created a parallel universe that allowed me to escape the harsh realities of the oppression I faced based on my gender, class and sexuality.

Although I was always a horrendous math and science student, I excelled at English, Languages and Social Studies. This ability helped me to gain entrance to an elite private school, where I evaded much of the in-your-face persecution I endured while in Elementary School and Junior High. My freshman year we wrote a letter to ourselves for a "time capsule" to be opened right before graduation four years later. In the letter, I asked myself, cryptically: "I wonder if it's still true…about things." In the intervening four years, I would spend hours scouring the academy library for anything pertaining to homosexuality, transvestism and transsexualism. I found some titles about being gay, but very little about gender-variance. I would take these books off the shelf and go search for an out-of-the-way study carrel to read every word I could on the subject, much of it outdated or medicalized, such as the work of John Money. I was too afraid and ashamed to ever check a book out about these subjects, terrified that someone would learn my deep, dark secret. Like many transpeople, I grew up thinking I was the only one in the world. Although I continued writing, I never talked about being queer or trans. In my junior year, I admitted to myself and my therapist that I was a transsexual. It felt so liberating to finally tell another human being, and be accepted as who I was.

Although the harassment dramatically decreased, I had difficulty making friends. I was a true loner and a geek who had trouble finding a social niche. I found some fellow outlaws in women of color students, many of whom came from urban environments. Transplanted to the lily-white world of the elite, private school, they too struggled to find acceptance and comfort in the face of overt and subtle racism. During my time there, the Ku Klux Klan became active in town and started to organize rallies, dressed in their full racist regalia. I took history and literature classes that examined the role of African Americans throughout history, and became outraged at the unending oppression that people of color have faced in the United States for over 500 years. Slowly but surely, my education and my interaction with diverse populations raised my critical consciousness and forced me to start asking some tough questions.

In addition to race, a whole other arena of oppression came into sharper view. I come from a blue-collar New Hampshire family; my mom worked as a hospital employee and my dad's a barber in the very town of this elite private school. We had to obtain scholarships, financial aid, and work study in order for me to attend the academy. From my freshman year, I started working: cleaning the library, working in the school cafeteria washing dishes and so fourth. I saw many of my classmates wearing the best clothes and never having to worry about money or finances. When they saw me working they were confused and asked me what I was doing. Many came from homes with personal servants, had vacationed all over the world, and had parents and grandparents who had attended the academy for generations before them. Classism, the institutional, cultural, and individual set of practices and beliefs that assign differential value to people according to their socio-economic class and the economic system which creates excessive inequality and causes basic human needs to go unmet, was illustrated to me at this juncture in my life. The more I read, and the more life I experienced, the more I began to see certain patterns continuously re-emerge, whether the category was race, class or gender.

In my freshman year at the University of New Hampshire, I continued to research transsexual issues and slowly started to pull open the closet door. I discovered that not only were there other people like me, but that they were organizing for change. Early on, I met brave trans pioneers who were proud of who they were and were trying to educate society about the realities of transpeople. Little did I know it at the time, but a remarkable and revolutionary movement was just getting started. The autonomous transgender liberation movement was giving birth to itself, and the world has not been the same since! From a terrified, gender-different kid being bullied in the corridors of junior high, I have matured into a fierce, self-styled transgender warrior. As a 6'6", queer, feminist, transgender, pagan, first-generation college student, working-class/economically-challenged, socialist, poet, Glamazon, I can usually count on someone somewhere having a problem with me. Throughout my undergraduate career and first graduate program, most of my writing was devoted to academic course work and to writing basic educational materials about gender issues. It was during my program in English Literature reading diverse types of literature that I decided: hey, I can try my hand at this, too! I decided that I was not only a reader of other people's works and a critic, but a creative writer myself.

Writing is not easy for me, and often not particularly joyful. I have an inner critic which constantly sits on my shoulder and tells me that what I write is not good enough, that it just doesn't measure up. Further, often what I write about is painful, and can bring up the many ghosts of my past and present. But nonetheless I write, and I will continue to write. What you now hold in your hands is the effort of nearly five years of work. It is authentic, heart-felt and real; it is, in the words of my Trans Mother Janice Josephine Carney, direct from a trans woman's soul. I often wear my emotions on my sleeve, and so, too, are they on blatant display in my poems. I believe that it is only through stark and even brutal honesty that we will ever begin to address the real problems that plague our society. Some of what you read may be difficult or even painful to hear. I respectfully ask that you process these words not in your brain alone, but in the eternally beating space of your heart. For through all of the differences we humans have, I always hold firm to the notion that we are more alike than unalike, and we can unify in ways that will shake the status quo to the foundation. I hope these poems challenge you, amuse you, anger you and move you. More than anything, I hope these poems find their way into the hands of a young or old person, who, like me, wanted to give up on life.

Early in my coming-out process, one of my parents told me that being an openly trans person was not worth it. I would face undue misery and hardship, and at the end of it all I would see that it was not worth the effort to challenge one of society's most sacred cows: gender. Dad was only partially right—I have indeed faced tremendous adversity and challenges. Sometimes I go through so many emotions in a single day that I lose count. I feel sadness so great that I want to crawl up in a fetal position and cry for days. Other times I feel rage and bitterness bubble inside me so strongly that I feel like my body will literally implode from the inside out. But one thing has not changed. I have never faltered in the belief that this struggle is worth it.

The Trans Army is joining together, one warrior at a time, and we will not stop until the Gender Revolution has been won. When I think of all my trans comrades who have fallen in battle, I am infinitely thankful for the chance to usher in another brilliant dawn. And I am grateful for the chance to write and to speak. I offer the words in this book as one more humble contribution to the creation of a radically different world. To my trans comrades who falter right now, whose eyes fill with tears, who feel ill-equipped to walk out of their house and face more derision, who have run out of opportunities, always remember how special you are to this world. There is not and never will be another you. And you, my friend, deserve to be here. And, as Audre Lorde always said: we ARE going to survive. So World, take note: the Gender Quake is ready to activate, and the whirl is gonna be blissful, and divine, and unstoppable.

I.
Trial by Fire:
Sissyhood Survivals

The First Poem

why so long
to put pen to paper?
years gone by, and pages left dusty and
blank
pens jammed full of ink.

it is almost summer now
an easier time perhaps
buried chest deep in snow
I needed to write a poem
gloom casting lingering shadows over me
racing, fleeing, tedious
heart-pounding maneuvers
but still no escape.

words offer little respite
spoken aloud they seem to
scatter and dissipate
as easily
as snowflakes.
written down, recorded on paper
they freeze into icicles
and I am trying hard to make sure
they do not shatter onto
unforgiving
pavement.

icicles are slippery
just like words.

in this, the First Poem,
how do I make my meaning
as clear as sky blue ice?

there is never such certainty,
in life or in word,

but it is better to try to
express, mark, record
even if that language
fails to register the
complexity, ambiguity and
radical diversity of
one's life.

I want my words to
sear through your memory
to assault you with color
my need to make words flourish like
neon pink pansies and
lavender lilies.

words and poems are seldom
so vibrant
but to scribble on a page
is at least as sweet smelling
as one soft, silken petal
radiantly beaming in the
sweltering sunlight
a patch of color to trick
my mind into high drive
a chance that it might be
worth the risk
after all.

so here it is:
clichés, bad similes and all
The First Poem.

I am not a Poet

I am not a poet.
my words are not well thought out,
concrete or vivid enough
evocative, emotional or poignant.

it is an ongoing painful struggle for me
arduous to try to see the beauty
they tell me
is all around me.
words do little to express
the never-ending hell
which constitutes the world.

and yes: I AM cynical.
for if I were not able to get angry
I probably would not survive.

I am not a poet.
too filled with constant outrage
flailing and rambling
a frustrated kook
who doesn't know when to shut up.

anger fills me like helium
in an outrageous orange balloon
pressing against the thin membrane
that is my skin and too often I go
POP!
      BAM!
          BAM!
POP!
the compressed air
exploding around me.
my orange flesh
shards of rubber on the grass.
and you—holding on to me—tightly,
sweating onto the string

warm palms pressed
not letting me fly free
even once.

I am not a poet.
I can't be aesthetic, pretty, beautiful,
words glowing with
sunshine brilliance.
everything I write becomes
a political tract
a manifesto, a plea,
a whine, or a whimper
and often a cry in the
fog-laden twilight.

grace is in short supply for me
I have a strange gait
I am "Too Tall" and funny-looking
bespectacled, misshapen and
often scowling.
I can't hide the gushing emotions
forcibly seizing my countenance and
scrambling all over the page
I bang my head nearly everyday
in doorways or buildings or buses or cars
resulting in an omnipresent
Concussion.
I am not overly hopeful that who I am,
what I say or the words I write
will hold appeal or sway in a
pretty, plastic world inhabited by
Barbies and Kens,
Chips and Buffies.

I am not a poet
I cannot change your mind
make you like me or
make you see beauty on this planet.

all I can do is assemble
letters, words and phrases
on terrifyingly blank scattered
white pages.
written in big girlish script
with little precision
direction or exact meaning
like countless other
Non-Poets
who nonetheless write their worlds
and guts out
all the while saying
I am not a Poet.

Some Entertaining Queens

Liberace
glitter, rhinestones, furs and pink poodle
buffed streaming cars
weighty beaming rings
as you hit endless piano keys.
So much flash but still you are safe,
Non-threatening.
To the end you kept silent,
about what everyone knew anyway.
Another life lost to that
ticking time-bomb called
Fear.

Richard Simmons
flitting around on TV
a constant infomercial
non-stop verbiage about nothing at all
a diet guru in
colored sequined tank tops,
daisy dukes and an afro.
If I see you benignly flirting with
David Letterman or your
omnipresent crocodile tears
one more time
I will SCREAM,
for real.

Elton John, another piano man
With endless variety of sunglasses,
tiaras and sappy songs that all sound the same.
So you came out and then sang with
Eminem on the Grammies,
even hugged him and
showed that he is a good guy.
Was your cheap publicity stunt worth it?
An antidote to sagging record sales?

Let the blood of hate crimes
be on your hands, sell-out.
Like Boy George said,
What you did is akin to him
Doing a duet with Pol Pot.
Oh so quick to sell queers down the river,
while you amass millions and build an
ever safer cocoon of ignorance.

Society wants its queens to be funny
and safe and innocent.
To mince, flounce, be fey
and ever so sweet and jolly
But where is the place for anger, rage,
OUT-rage?

I am a tree,
tall and unswerving
Angry and Vengeful
Do not take my queeniness for easiness
I am difficult and proud of it
Shouting, running,
swinging against the tide
I do not exist to make you laugh
or feel comfortable
to cement your ill-begotten illusions.
I am tearing down closet doors,
speaking uncomfortable truths
unchaining a long legacy of
Queenly subordination.

To those "entertaining" queens, I say:
I am not the straight world's stooge
I do not exist to entertain or
be an Aunt Thomasina
My anger is a spider web
Sticky, massive and growing
Catching bigotry with

venomous nerve
Both my own and yours
Climbing around endlessly
My limp wrist
quickly transformed into a
Clenched Fist.
I will not get caught in your
web of deception.

So to Elton, Richard,
and other phony queens I state:
What is the politics behind your posturing?
Your queenliness is just another
masculine mask,
a femmy-façade
caked in crackling foundation and
smeared mascara.

With heels, hair and attitude,
I stand Seven Feet Tall.
I am stomping those stilettos through the ground,
perpetually marching forward
Sashaying to amuse myself,
not to curry favor with those who despise me.
Fiercely yelling and screaming my pain,
piercing through the night air.

Rage in your face!

Some Words About People

Some of the kindest people I know
are also some of the loneliest.

Some of the smartest people I know
are bereft of intellectual engagement.

Some of the saddest people I know
have the most potential for true joy.

Some of the strongest people I know
are vulnerable inside straight to the core.

Some of the most together people I know
inside are crumbling down to bone dust.

Some of the calmest people I know
have a fire erupting inside their gut.

Some of the prettiest people I know
look in the mirror and see barren ugliness.

Some of the richest people I know
don't have a proverbial pot to piss in.

Some of these people are me.
Are any of these people you?

Inner Child

What did the bullies rob from me
on the playground?
How did they silence my spirit?
They squashed a young femme's desire for
prettiness, loveliness and unending color
in an ugly world
Spit on, beaten, pushed around
was merely the physical
Much more damaging was the verbal
searing through ghostly pansy skin
words endlessly eaten
bitter tastes always resurfacing
and in my own passivity
trembling with pathetic fear
for like many I was un-armed
parents who would rather see me
Disappear
then own up to the depths of my
Perverse Queerness
parents whose tongues would
unfurl blame and hostility
for it was not the world's fault,
but my
Own.

And the saddest part is that
I believed them.
for a very, very long time.
And I still struggle to break free
of the fierce
Shame
shackled like a worshipful dog,
still hoping that something
anything I do
will make them like me, respect me,
Be proud of me.

See
the bullies on the playground
that's only half the story
the greatest pain emanates from within
and is much harder to heal
I can hate myself more than they ever
Hated me.
and therein lies the most insidious threat
learning to swallow the poisonous pills
One after another,
leading slowly, but surely, to death.
a shy, sensitive, bespectacled book worm,
I still mourn for that sissy boy
Never given a moment's peace
Never allowed to simply exist
but even more I mourn for every
gender queer child
every different kid
those who live on an entirely different
plane of being
who grow up to hate the
unique selves that they are.

Great Mother Goddess,
With the Strength and Fury of the ages
Grant us the Self-Esteem,
Self-Respect and
Self-Love we need to
grow and prosper on this planet.
Let us not contribute to our own
un-doing and
destruction.
Let us learn to parent our inner child
And save that sweet, innocent, playful and
Child-Ful
aspect of own being.
Let all those brave, different kids

coming up be spared
the wounds we now carry on into adulthood.
Let us forgive our parent's mistakes
and never carry them over to another generation.
And let us find that one scene, or place, or episode
in our childhood when we felt genuine joy
unadulterated Pleasure in
Be-ing.
unsullied by cultural norms or societal flaws.

Like the "me" at age five
I dressed as little red riding hood
and won first prize for best costume and
developed a life-long love for the
bewitching day of
Halloween.
Or those long walks along Hampton Beach
with Mom and Grammy when gender didn't matter.
Only the roaring of the waves pounding the surf
Or Grammy's dog Mandy happily smelling in the sand.
And the development of another love:
the solace found in staring into the depths of the Sea.

Small fragments of solace and hope
memories to guide me on a path of
righteous self-love
ending lethal doses of internal disgust
healing me onward to an
immortal journey of loving freedom
and self-communion.

Hate

Hate begets hate
It is never late
Splattered crimson
All over my fate.

Words poised to kill
Or create a quick thrill
Another empty hole
To temporarily fill.

When he calls me a fag
There ain't barely a lag
I want to return to him
A premeditated jag.

When she calls me a bitch
Honey, it's time to switch!
Ready to grab her by the arms
And hurl her in a ditch.

On this journey called life
I carry a sharp knife
With bitterness and indignation
I am constantly rife.

See, rage is all over my page
It is never hard to gauge
The need in me to shriek through the night
And go on a revenge-filled rampage.

You'd think by now I'd be more Sage.

But:

Hate begets hate
It is never late
Splattered crimson
All over my fate.

Boyhood Tears

For Janice-My Beloved Trans Mom

Sitting side by side
in the darkened movie theatre
watching *Mystic River*
we watched boys struggle with fear,
with the shackles of masculinity
forced onto tender childhood flesh
and we, two strong proud transwomen,
Mother and Daughter
cried boyhood tears.

In your cozy Florida living room
I hear you talk about your time in Vietnam
that haunted year that will never fully
disappear
and how they tried to make a man out of you
beaten, bloodied and bullied in
tough Boston high schools
You fly thousands of miles to Vietnam:
a baby face
but they make you shave daily
until the hair grows in thick and noticeable
for the baby drag queen
the femme boy
the baby face forever lost
we cry
boyhood tears.

Years later, married and the father of
a young boy
you wake up nightly plagued by the
ghosts of Vietnam
You try to reach out to your son
but something blocks you
a prisoner of a scarred past

encased in the jail of society's
cold manhood
for your son's hurt and alienation
we cry
boyhood tears.

For our father's coldness
cruelty and simmering rage
for alcohol-breath-words-of-hate
for hands and belts used to hurt us
for them not being there
even when they are
sitting right in front of us
we cry
boyhood tears.

Here we stand in the gentle ocean waters
two strong proud transwomen
Mother and Daughter
Hand in Hand
still mourning for the boys
that were not allowed to
Be.

For every young femme princess today
Cursed and spit on at the playground
Forced to take off her rainbow hair barrette,
her pink lipstick or her glitter nail polish
taught to hate herself and
forced to conform
For all those vibrant baby faces
yet to be sliced by the blade of
society's callous and
monochrome
cruelty
we cry
boyhood tears.

For the Boy that I Was

I learned about gender on the playground
       Teased mercilessly for being a sissy

Gender became a trial by fire
       "You can't do this! You can't do that!"

I mourn for the boy that I was
       A shy, sensitive boy who was never
allowed to exist in peace

A boy who liked flowers more than football
       Glitter more than guns
Blowing bubbles more than bragging

For this they called me faggot, queer, girly boy
       My crime? Being different
Head lowered in shame and endless tears

But now I am grown
       And I have gotten stronger

You tried to kill the queer girly-boy in me
       But you did not succeed

I reach back through time and space and
hug my childhood self tightly and say:
       No one can extinguish your flaming passions
       Your ferocious femme-y ways
To the shy, sensitive boy that I was I say
       THANK YOU.
I say: You deserve a long, happy life.
       I say: I LOVE YOU.

II.
Casualties of Gender:
Re-Membering Fallen S/heroes

Venus: Goddess of Love

For Venus Xtravaganza

petite and platinum blond,
sashaying and sassin' down the runway
the glimmer in your eyes reach into my own
walking down mean New York streets,
reading and throwing shade with your sisters,
give 'em hell girl,
your hope is infectious
I feel an unexplainable connection to you
my sister,
my own story reflected back at me
I hope we do not meet the same end,
but know we could.

what did he do to you those last hours of your life
as you struggled to survive?
What did you feel inside while he used and
fucked you like a rag-doll,
the hands tightening around your neck,
leaving purple thumb marks on your light skin?
till the end I see you struggling to live
for we are survivors,
whether we live or
die.

Venus, Goddess of Love,
my amazing strong sister wo/man,
what were your last thoughts as you left this world?
the last thing you saw, the last thing you heard?
did you ever fully realize the power and beauty that was
inside yourself all along?
Did you ever really feel the love you
deserved?

The beast that plucked the pulse

from your veins,
did he realize all your never-ending
struggles and heartaches?
The pain, ostracism, abuse, rejection
that pummeled your body again and again?
The words that seared through your thin skin
like burning flames,
that boiled your crimson blood?

he strangled the physical life out of you and
left you to die like gender trash on the floor
of a sleazy New York City hotel
for days you rotted as your body lay motionless
on the grime-covered floor

But Venus, your spirit escaped that dismal hotel room
I know because you have visited me in my dreams
You take me by the hand and remind me that
I will never, ever be alone again

The thug that so viciously drained the life out of you
couldn't rob your spirit
it fills me and all the other Queens and Princesses,
validates us and affirms our absolute right to
a place on this vast earth

Venus, Goddess of Love,
beat down by your gender,
beat down by who you loved,
beat down by your color,
beat down by your poverty,
the richness of your soul sings to me and
pushes me forward into the promise of a
radiant new morning.

I hope you know that nary a day goes by
that I do not think of the dead
Trans Spirits lining the

journey of my path.
We are different and we are the same
Venus
hatred and injustice killed you
and it is Love and Justice
that will save us
All of Us.

The Rape of Brandon Teena

"I've been so lost lately I can't even cry."

We honor the dead by
Re-Membering them,
by memorializing their essence.

They held you and refused to let you move.
They stripped your pants off to display your
genitals to the world.
They had to know what you were.
They said your life was one big lie.
You deceived, posed as a man,
seduced innocent straight girls.
Your crime was being a
          gender
                    outlaw.

They held you in the backseat of a
bitterly cold
Nebraska winter,
Christmas Eve, 1993.
They took turns raping you to make a
twisted point,
to set you "straight."
After the horror you reported it to
Sheriff Laux.
This time the rape was more insidious,
accomplished through words and innuendo.

"Do you run around with a sock in your underpants?"

"He doesn't fondle you any, huh?
Doesn't that amaze you?"

"So when they get ready to poke you
how was you positioned in the back seat?"

"Where did they try to pop in first at?"

"Did he have a hard-on when
he got back there or what?"

"Did you have to work it up for him?"

Your friend said your
worst fear
was to be raped.
And it happened.

It happened more than once.

They called the perpetrator a faggot for raping you.
The perpetrator's girlfriend says
he is not a faggot because he raped a girl.

You voice on the police tape is shaking.
Your terror and pain on full display.

In pictures you have a gleaming style
A baby face,
close-cropped brown hair,
a delicate countenance.

After they raped you,
your mom said you had already died.

But your tormentors were not satisfied.
They returned to a lonely farmhouse in the
ghastly twilight
and pumped you full of bullets.
Your mom said there was
no place on your head
that did not have bumps.
Blood smeared all over the wall
And they killed the young single mother

who was giving you shelter and they
killed the African American disabled man, too.

Later the perpetrator called you
two dykes and a nigger.
Unworthy of life at all.

They only spared the baby,
nine months old and
screaming in the back room.

Your gravestone says Teena R. Brandon
Daughter, Sister, Friend.

Even in death they must gender you.
Even after your death they say your life was one big lie.

I write these words to search for truth.

And I write these words because
we honor the dead by
Re-Membering them.

Unidentified Transvestite Male

Shot execution style.
Multiple stab wounds.
Strangled.
Gang raped.
Sodomized.
Beaten. Slapped. Kicked.
Left to die.
Buried in a shallow grave.

We know some of your names:
Brandon, Amanda, Gwen, Stephanie,
Ukea, Rita, Debra, Fredericka.

But others remain:
Nameless
Faceless
Voiceless.

Unidentified transvestite male.
Man found dead wearing wig.

I think of you, my unknown sister,
lying motionless
blood rivulets flowing from slashed-open skin
decaying in a puddle of crimson.
the twilight sidewalk
glistening with fresh rain droplets
the luminance of the moon
casting eerie shadows
on your battered anonymous
Body.

Your wig,
so a part of your identity,
tipped off your head,
lying sodden in a

cigarette-butt laden puddle,
mixing with traces of your
blood.

How do I resurrect you?
How do I learn who you were?
What you liked to eat?
What you liked to talk about?
How you liked to dress?
And, especially, what were your dreams?
Who did you hope to become?
And what kind of world
did you hope to give birth to?

When I see, buried deep in the newspaper,
or typeset in a gay magazine,
or flickering out in cyberspace
"unidentified transvestite male"
my own emotions betray me
tears eke from the corners of my eyes
and I want more than anything to
give up on this world
this hate-filled world
where people like you
never had a chance
where people like us
were never meant to survive
where enough blood has been
violently shed to fill
an
Ocean.

But when the tears dry
I stare at the words again,
and feel my blood spurting through my veins
my pulse quickening
tangible proof that I am
Alive

and I make a pact with myself
I will fight for you my
Nameless
Faceless
Voiceless
Sisters
Scream, Yell, Chant, Picket and Complain
until god-damn-it somebody listens!
Until you have in death
what you never had here:
Peace
and
Respect.

There is, Always

For Jesse

we met at a transgender rap group
the two youngest people present
we slipped out early into the
misty Seattle Evening
and went back to my place
to bask in the newly-found glow of
Recognition

weeks later I call you and you are
dejected, depressed, devoid of
Hope.
your boyfriend has come home to
find you passed out in the shower,
multiple slash wounds to your neck
a victim of your own sabotaging hand
it is not your first attempt, but your tenth
and when I see you again I finger the pink,
fleshy wounds and scars,
the tangible proof of Your,
Our,
Open Pain
wounds gaping with terror,
the hate they fling at us like
shit
internalized and leading straight to
self-destruction.

you ask me: What is There?
at the time I stammered
tongue searching for words in vain
words to lay claim to our shame,
our fear,
our broken dreams

years later, I do not know where you are,
or even if you are Alive.
if you have survived the baseball bat of the basher
The time bomb of AIDS
the terror of drug and alcohol addiction or that
slashing hand which seeks its own version of freedom,
release,
peace.
A permanent Ending to the terror.

My words have not improved much
over these years,
but when you asked me pointedly and truthfully—
What is There?
I wish I had told you this.

There is always a kind stranger somewhere,
appearing out of long corridors,
on dark street corners,
with a nod of approval,
a simple smile
a question of genuine caring.

There is always another pulsating
grooving song
sonic aid to the spirit
or a freewheeling gyrating dance,
a free-zone of bodily possibilities,
spiraling carelessly,
moving magically,
to enliven the soul
and reinvigorate the blood.

There is always the
Word.
Spoken and Written,
forever imperfect,

but a blade in the side of the enemy,
used to blind-side bigots,
subvert domination,
punch out prejudice
endlessly, enduring words
wreak havoc and aid in our
Survival.

There is always another
Laugh
Somewhere,
(though you may have to search long and hard)
Queenly and Flamboyant,
Sisterly and Sinister
endless peals of laughter,
high pitched haughty homos,
laughing at absurdity
flatly refusing to stop.

There is always a sister,
even if only in your dreams
a warm hand on your back, rubbing
away the layers of grimy pain
believing in us against the odds,
even when we cannot believe in
Ourselves.

There is always a dream,
a vision,
a hope.
not a maudlin fantasy,
but a carefully conceived blueprint,
a radical dream of a different time and place,
where equality rules the day and
oppression is no longer in sight.

BUT, without doubt, and most importantly,
There is always YOU.

Short and sassy,
blond and bubbly,
sweet and snappy,
smart beyond your years
braver than most, bolder than many.
And there is no one like you.
And you, my friend,
deserve to be
Here.

These are only a few reasons to stay alive
I have missed so many,
and only you can shade in the rest
Fill in the blanks and teach me sister
But when you asked me: What is There?
I can only say this:
There Is ....
Always.

III.
Warriors I Have Known

Dawn

For Donald Osgood

I do not know where to begin, my sister
Maybe in that dark, dreary gay bar,
where I walked in dazed and
before I knew what hit me:
There you are!
Bouncing, laughing, queening-out and
can't stop
Girlfriend! You are back!
It's been nearly four years since
I've last laid eyes on you.
You look radiant, your eyes glittering
green and gray,
wide-set and intent upon surviving and thriving.

But your joyous expression belies a deeper-set
pain and anguish.
Your ex-boyfriend is gone,
jailed for molesting teenaged boys,
but you have an even more exacting
prison sentence:
he infected you with
HIV.

My mind reels back ten years,
to your head being crashed into a locker,
to being hunted like an animal by teen boys
intent on killing your spirit.
And I think back to what you have told me:
raped, molested numerous times,
abused by ex-boyfriends.
You grew up working class,
deep up north in the mountains.
A "half-breed" who learned
what you could about your
Native Heritage.

Scrubbing toilets and sinks,
making endless beds in tourist hotels,
just like your mother had before you.

I flash back to reality on the dance floor
I extend one extra-long, queenly arm and
flip my wrist
Then snap my fingers
Despite untold abuse,
you have come back into my life
Sashaying and reading and giggling.
You have several names:
Don, Donald, Onny, Donnatella
But I think I like Dawn best
Like the crimson-violet-orange burst
You keep on arisin' each morning
to bear in a new day
Despite being queer,
abused,
HIV +,
you are intent on living your life,
unstoppable and thirsty for freedom.

Like a true home-girl,
you call or more often
drop by unannounced
and I grumble my:
"Think you could have called first?"
But inside I don't want you to call.
I want you to come, sit and shoot the shit.
Smoking and drinking screwdrivers,
Delirious dishing, dissin' and debate
After you leave I feel better about
being in this world,
less alone and less afraid.
Your spirit rubs off on me
in ways you don't
Realize.

You are called many names:
Don, Donald, Onny, Donnatella
But I think I like Dawn, best.

My androgynous sister,
I see the rising sun in you
Defiantly daring to rise
Uproariously challenging me to
do better and go further
And never allowing the blackest of nights
to cease you from glittering,
sprinkling rhinestones all over your
uncertain path.

We go way back, you tell me so often.
Yes, Sister.
And we are gonna go
way forward, too.

Morbidity

Walking through the graveyard at midnight
the witching hour
I catch a glimpse of the
Goddess's face in the
Luminous Moon.

You are at my side, and tell me to
return here after you die,
to think of you and invite
your Spirit to come back to me.

HIV is ticking away inside your blood,
and I do not care to ponder its
possible pumping endpoint
even here
amidst the decay of many thousands
rotting away in the ground.

I feel peace for the first time in months
the moonlight sweetly caressing us
the joy of a sister
the recognition of a home-girl
peals of laughter
slicing humid August air
souls reviving at midnight
confidant in the comfort of each other's
Care.

Later you move hours away
and when I pass the graveyard I think about:
You and Morbidity and Me.
And the omnipresent blood.
The ubiquitous threat.
I see crimson handprints on
ancient gravestones.
Everyone, Everything,

Dying all around us.
All of the time.
Life's only certainty.

The Goddess in the Moon
Beckoning
to You and To Me.

All in Good Time,
All in Good Time.

Two Trees

For Allison

Two tall narrow
Trees
Shooting up, skyward.
Barren and brittle
Thin outstretched branches
Ever ready to snap in the wind.

Our soil is eternally dry
Our roots shallow and sickly
Permanent clouds blocking our sun
Only an occasional ray darts through
With busts of orange radiance.

No one bothers to water us much
Or give us the light and warmth we crave
Two slighted trees
Struggling to
Grow.

Maybe we can make our branches intertwine
Help each other to stand
Strong
Our roots meshing together
A lush, sun-drenched remedy to two
Love-Deprived
Trees
Shooting up, skyward.

Slice

White Mounds of mashed potatoes
Lovingly prepared.
Brown gravy, piping hot,
No lumps.
Bright green shining peas
Tossed with circular pearl onions.
Cranberry sauce, a gelatinous mass
Perfectly slid from can to plate.
White rolls from the oven
Awaiting pats of butter.
Autumn butternut squash
Orange, with just a dash of cinnamon.
And the Pièce de la Résistance:
The Turkey.
Sliced, white, breast meat.
Bow your heads and say grace.
Be grateful, obedient and
enjoy the meal.
Eat the meal and have
pleasant, innocuous conversations.
Slice the turkey. And then—
Sister's wrists.
Sliced.
Fresh, multiple slash wounds.
Criss-crossing each other on left and right wrists.
Almost covered by shirt sleeves.
Avert eyes.
Pour gravy on potatoes.
Slice the turkey.
Slice the wrist.
Eat Pie!
Pumpkin with vanilla ice cream.
Happy Turkey Day
From my American family
to yours.

Junior High

For Dana

I eyeballed you at lunch one day
sitting across from me at "Table 3"
reserved for the freaks.
retards.
poor white trash and other
assorted riff raff.

you had an afro then that framed your face
and you were tall and wore glasses like me
you were a droplet of coffee in a
sea of homogenized milk
but we didn't talk about that then.

For the short duration of lunch,
we ate, chatted and let the surroundings
melt away—a welcome respite.

No, it wasn't until years later that
I learned about the trauma you endured.

gangs of white boys
chasing you through the trailer park
punching, kicking, tripping
Terrorizing.

They tried to rape you,
and humiliated and degraded you.
the words
"nigger" and "bitch"
echoing endlessly
from well-heeled white children,
society's pride and joy.
an unresolved orbit sent through your
brain tissue

and I did not know your anguish then
the way you wanted to die
that you tried to end your
Life.

I did not know of your home life
mostly shut inside your bedroom in the trailer
heavy metal music blaring
one way to blot out the pain
tears glistening as you plotted
your escape.

15 years later,
the line cracks over a thousand miles
distance
but the pain is as present and alive as a
thudding heartbeat
but, I want to remind you
through the thicket of dagger-like thorns
we met and became friends
two burgundy roses
frosted but vibrant
pushing up audaciously in
a cemetery of
Dreams that are
chopped and broken like centuries-old
headstones.

So, sage sister,
through the velvet-draped haze
of foggy memories
remember to see me hovering,
always within whispering range
Protecting your Spirit.

Love and sisterhood born out of
Chaos.
Enduring, abiding,

forged in spite of and in resistance to
hatred and self-hatred.

Two burgundy roses in
a cemetery of
Dreams
thorns deadly after years of
steadfast sharpening.

We won't let them hurt us anymore.

No More Sleepless Nights

For Janice

"In World War II the average age of the combat soldier was 26.
In Vietnam he was 19."   - "19" by Paul Hardcastle

Listening alone in my apartment to the song "19"
Our country on the verge of war once again
I think of my adopted Mother
My Tranny Mama
And reflect on her life.

Returning from Vietnam
She never received a hero's welcome
She was spit on, cursed at and denied jobs,
called a baby killer.
I mourn for the oh-so-young baby queen
Turned loose on the mean streets of Boston
Trying to find a way to survive.

For so many years
You chased the woman in you away
Drowned her out in omnipresent bottles of
Jack Daniels.

Like many other Vietnam Veterans
You continued to fight the Vietnam War,
long after you returned to these shores.

How many sweat-filled nights of terror?
How many sleepless nights?
How many others faced the same fate,
who are all but lost to history?
How many ended the anguish
at their own hand or tried to?

When I look at the TV
Shouting about "Showdown with Saddam"
I wonder: have we learned our lesson?
Have we forgot the 58,000 Vietnam Vets
who were slaughtered and the ones
who fought for basic dignity
when they returned?

I mourn for John: a young and beautiful
Princess
Destroyed by childhood rape
Beaten down by cruel young men
Spoiled by the hellishness of war
S/he never had a chance to be.

But now you are Janice Josephine
and you have found a way to be free:
You:
My Elder, my Mother, my Friend.
Shining with a luminescence.
Like the moon,
You fill me with light.
You changed your body
to let Janice gleam with
Brilliance.
And through the wisdom of the Goddess,
I know you are like the woman
I wish to become.

But still I worry, sometimes
Late at night
I venture outside in the
cold New England winter
and look up into
an onyx nightscape
Glittering with stars.

And wish for you what I wish for myself,
indeed for the whole world:
Eternal peace.
And I hope that,
a thousand miles away,
in the warmth of a distant
Florida night
That you are dreaming of
chasing butterflies in Costa Rica
And that you never again have
      Another
         Sleepless
           Night.

IV.
The Edges of Hope and Despair

Bus Ride

what does one do
when one's head is bursting apart at the
seams?
silver spikes split into brain tissue
rammed from right side to left
skewered with intellectual gush
because my mind swims restlessly, and
I imagine lightning rods
splitting the ceiling
of the bus
and sparking the metal rods.
silencing the lush moody Cure songs
flowing through my
impenetrable ear phones

I am surrounded by glum faces.
we are the unlucky ones
without our own steel metal box
set atop a set of four impervious wheels
so we worship together in a bigger box
barely acknowledging each other's
existence
but bounded together
nonetheless
in grimy steel
and droplets of sweat
and bittersweet
unshed tears

a 3" opening provides
room for my hand to
escape
rushes of air
streaming through open slender
Fingers
signs endlessly rush by

blurring reality
a 3-D movie screen to numb the
stark truth sitting right in front of us
what the theorists call
post-industrial
late capitalism
this fractured
postmodern world

I feel a sudden chill and
slam the window
shut.
I take a heady whiff of alienation,
breathe in the last drops
of grim determination,
and delight in the feeling of the metal rods
puncturing my eyeballs.

Iowa

setting down from a glacial sky
11:00 at night
the clipped baritone from the
cockpit announces:
twenty degrees below zero
I shudder as I scramble
to get off and find a phone
clips of paper, torn and ragged
held to fluorescent light
beeps mashing from fingertips
"Hi, you have reached 319..."
answering machine, voice mail, no answer.
I whack the phone back to the receiver
scurrying through the small
Cedar Rapids airport
I ask a red faced man about vans
"Leaves in an hour."
I'm told my luggage is missing as
I get lost
in the endless rows of
black and beige
and navy blue rectangles
sitting, ownerless.

waiting for the van to pull up
freezing beyond the arctic.
there are three other passengers.

en route, I look across the
Iowa plains and see a
blue white glacier that never ends
an interminable stillness
electric shining frost
the silence in the van only as palpable
as my
Loneliness.

we drop off a teenaged boy first
who struggles not to slip as he lugs a
huge red duffle bag to the
illuminated front door,
his father hugging him as he enters.

then we drive for another hour,
for the next destination, and
I am oblivious to time or direction
snow shimmying across the black air,
wipers scrambling to clear the glass.

when I am finally alone with
the old driver,
he can't find my apartment.
circling around campus,
snow flutters and sways in spurts,
highlighted by bright street lamps.
I hand him a tip and cavort up the stairs
to my pitch black apartment.
eyeing my enormous snow-prints
with each step
baggage-less, but still bearing
the weight of 200
Psychic Tons.

Peering out my tiny kitchen window,
I wonder what I am doing
in this place
at this time.

And revert to childhood prayers:
I ask for a snow angel to swoop in
        and love me
                and fly away with me

and take me away from this cold
        lonely place
                forever.

Sex Change Dream

Joseph strangles the turkey's neck
Milks the final estrogen-laden drops
And smears them on the mini statue of
Christ by the bed.

The surgeon's table is ice cold
Gleaming silver metal.
The blade gingerly makes contact with skin
Slicing away decades of shame
Scissoring off grief
Chopping off self-hatred
The doctor is finally freeing her
Granting gender serenity.
The joy of entering the world afresh.
And free. And happy.

The stitches still fresh
The pain non-existent
Only the full-body glow of
Gender Euphoria.

She digs a hole on the white house lawn
In this country called
AmeriKKKa
And gleefully buries her own
Rotting balls.

She plants a single white rose
And bids adieu to Joseph
For all eternity.

No More Courage

what happens when my wrist cramps up
and I can no longer write?
my pen out of ink,
my soul out of blood.

what happens when my portable CD player
stops spinning my tunes?
my ears deaf to the spirit of an artist's
musical love.

what happens when the dance
abruptly stops?
my limbs limp and lifeless
folding in on myself like a limp cloth
disintegrating into a puddle on the
star-laden floor.

what happens when dawn
never comes?
the sun stubbornly refusing to rise
my ears nailed shut as I long to slumber for eternity,
this my only peace.

what happens when I feel zapped
of every emotion—
sadness, anger, hope, and despair?

what happens when I feel nothing left to cling to
when one final pair of raping eyes breaks
through to that inviolable place in my soul?

will you be there to hold me up?
to pull the TransAmazon from
hir crumpled ball on the floor?

to hold my cold, clammy hand and
push warmth back into my pulsating heart?

to pull open my eyeballs and
scrape off the crusted blood?

to unhinge my ears so I can
hear again, listen again?

to refresh my limbs
so I can dance again?

to witness one more
majestic pink-orange sunrise?

will you be there for me
when there is
No More Courage?

Layers

black slacks, black sweater, black coat,
black shoes, black socks, black hat,
black gloves, black scarf.

my body: an impenetrable charcoal fortress.
A tree glowering against one too many
frigid New England
Twilights.
Inside my blood boils,
freezes, pumps with fury, rage,
and deep
Abiding Sadness.
can my visage possibly signal the
flow inside my veins?
Can the trickle from my
nose give a faint clue?
I am invulnerable,
controlled,
purely academic.

I've gotta hold it together
Be Coherent
oblivious to the arctic wind
contained and shadey as a
New Hampshire forest
not open and exposed
like a vast, Midwestern prairie

but some people have tricky
EYES
they see through layers ever so quickly
see through the obsidian glass shield
to the quivering hysterical mass
that by sheer force of will
will not splinter or shatter or
explode.

on an interminable black night
where icicles hang like exquisite sky sculptures
and stars shimmer off your iridescent eyes
I may turn to you and surprise you
peel off the layers.
Are you ready to see?

Alone Again

my roommate moved out
school is done for the summer
I sit in my apartment, a converted old mill,
and listen to the water rush endlessly
outside.

the air is dense and stagnant,
eerily inert.
I wait listlessly for the phone
to rudely ring
and intrude onto my
elaborate illusions.

It does not.

instead, silences pierces me,
and my aloneness presses though
thin skin membranes and
pours bitter into crimson blood
inserts itself into bone density
cuts through endless fleshy organs.

aloneness, isolation,
loneliness, alienation.
These things I know like
dawn and sunset,
the need for food and water.
the daily mundane feeling of
just me,
again.

it is a sentiment that us
trans women know all too well.
yes, I have friends.
but there are large gaps without
calls, emails, visits.

and I must look at myself in the mirror,
gaze deeply into worn-out eyes and
declare my rage
(but that is on more hopeful days)

if I can stay mad,
surviving feels as tangible
as a plump orange quarter
exploding onto my tongue.
releasing sweetness and
relieving my thirst,
replenishing and quenching
my need to feel

Alive.

but today it is unmitigated
sadness,
falling over me in
endless vertical shadows,
cloaking me like black velvet drapes
in an ailing funeral home.

straight up gloom and bitterness,
anger at being alone again,
and no resolve or knowledge of
how to transform this
weight of constant
one-ness,
this reality of
just-me-ness.

the more I live,
the more I begin to see
isolation in very
Political Terms.
As an uppity, angry, militant
Gender Outlaw

solitary confinement is an
extreme form of
Punishment.
prisoners, the elderly, the differently-abled,
the freaks,
all get flushed down the social toilet,
left to contend with everyone else's shit.

people staying clear of me
is a subtle way to try to
destroy me,
or drive me crazy,
or make me hate myself.

this is not usually an active ploy,
but a passive one which is just as
effective.

now I do know why so many of my sisters
get lost in a maze of alcoholism and drugs,
a haze of prostitution,
anonymous sex.
anything to kill the pain of constant,
unceasing loneliness,
an aloneness that shoots
through the body with
undeniable force.

So,
Alone Again,
I must decide to be
Angry Again.
A piss poor alternative,
to be sure,
but better to be pissed off and bitter
and maybe even disliked
than permanently and unalterably
dead.

Psycho Tropics

It's vacation time
And I'm off to the
Psycho Tropics
For a little R & R
Transparent orange bottles lined up
Pushed into the pristine white sand
Xanax and Wellbutrin and Prozac
Attivan and Paxil and Remeron
Zoloft and Klonopin and Trazedone
Celexa and Effexor and Serizone.
I press my belly into the sand and
methodically pop open the lids.
The pills are little citrus candies
Lime green and tangerine orange
Raspberry pink and coconut white
I gather them with my hand and
Gouge them all into my mouth
Teeth shattering into bitter fruit
Beads of sweat pouring forth from
every pore.
The water serenely
pressing against the surf,
Eventually washing away the bottles
Pills thrown into the air like
colored raindrops
And I fall asleep.
In the Psycho Tropics
Peaceful
And
Happy! ☺
At last.

I. A T-Girl's Dilemma

a silk purple scarf
fluttering out into the wind
you stand fixing your
striking lipstick named
"Carnal"
a study in unconventional beauty
a long stemmed crimson rose
blooming passionately in a field of snow.

you do not notice me pondering you
the first sister I've seen in months
your hair spiraling carelessly
the hem of your skirt billowing
my heart pulsating with desire
to connect, to eradicate the
Void
momentarily
but with the very next heartbeat
you start to walk away.
Fleeing through the mist into
that world you and
I dare to exist in.

looking out into the gathering clouds
I feel the blood begin to drain from my body
peeking out in plump droplets
then streaming out through multiple pores

Is this the punishment
for those of us who mange to survive?
this feeling of bloodless alienation?
a loneliness that penetrates the bone
a dread that splices through infinitesimal
cells, and endless fragmentation that
pokes through
every sticky organ?

dripping with red syrup my mind
contemplates HER/HIR/HIM
my strange and intimate queer sister
questions race through my brain:
Will you find light? Peace? Love?
Will you evade knives, fists, and bullets?
Will your spirit withstand verbal violence,
words piercing empty twilights to the grave?
Will you see 30 more years? 10?
Even 1?
and through those long, listless years,
will the struggle all be worth it
at the mythical
end?

shivering and coated with blood I wonder:
how will we stem the interminable flow?
and how will we sop it up?

II. A T-Girl's Prayer

the gleaming white porcelain tub
crimson petals floating
warm water lulling and inviting
ME,
cajoling my
red-stained body,
blood now caked in unsightly smears
submerging myself,
I let the water do its work
a cleansing deeper than the vast level of
skin
a soulful purification,
much needed warmth to balm my essence

ending the spirit shivers.

on the table by the tub,
I light one small white candle,
and begin to gaze listlessly into its
eternity
swearing off thoughts for
clarity
from the
everyday goddesses I invoke
who've seen me though the
journey this far.

I see the carnal lips and spiraling hair fade
into my mind,
a shining transgender princess,
standing not in mist, but surrounded by
triangles of light
flickering specks of
brilliance.

eyes closed,
petals floating,
candle bravely burning,

I pray to you, my sister, as to myself,
neither unrecognized nor unknown.

Great Goddesses,
Mothers of us all:

GRANT US
Light and clarity:
the ability to know and see ourselves.
To look in mirrors and feel
love and power.

GRANT US
Wisdom and common sense.
The ability to know who to trust.
The know-how to survive the
world's daily
Brutalities

GRANT US
Connection and sisterhood.
For if we do not stand,
joined together in infinite chains,
we will not survive.
Help us to see each other,
as we see ourselves,
reflected in your infinite beauty.

GRANT US
Perseverance and Resolve.
when all else falls apart,
grant us the fight back spirit of
Generations
Many Strong and Mighty Warriors

Amazons All
Fighting back against injustice.
Fists raised in righteous solidarity,
Unfaltering
Waiting for yet another
explosion of dawn
pink orange sunshine rays
Reminding us of your POWER
the power that is always already
inside
Ourselves.

soaking in stillness
I open my eyes
and turn to the candle and gaze
Steadfastly.
My body is now free of blood,
my mind still and calm
I rise slowly from the water
my clean body soft and tender
And stare intently into the
steam covered mirror.
I take my finger and
Slowly
Painstakingly
Write my Own
Name.

Snow Suicide

trudging uphill
bundled in black layers
steely blue eyes
gazing at winter
Twilight.

cars swerve because I am
Unseeable
a charcoal ghost
unleashed on an
onyx evening.

but in the snow I am a
raven
flittering like a lunatic
unhinged in frigid glaciers
shivering onto interminable
white
wanting to sink into pearlized
warmth
layers of radiance.

Committing
snow suicide.

Instead,
I tromp forward.

Quivering into the frigid
Lunar Glow.

V.
Standing (6'6") Tall:
A TransAmazon's Empowerment

My Power Poem

"Your Voice is Too Loud!"
"You're So Overpowering!"
"You are Really, Really Tall!"
"You Seem So Angry!"

To these frequent charges I respond:

My voice is not loud enough
My falsetto may fool you at first
But not for long
My voice, my words, are my survival
I speak loudly because, being invisible,
It is the only prayer I have of being heard,
or, better yet,
Listened to.

When my voice is loud, it is because
I am passionate and engaged
Trying to speak out the pain, terror,
anguish and rage which haunt me
and the occasional joy and satisfaction
which court me.

Given the injustice and despair
all around us
We should all be louder!
Screaming against oppression
Crying out for the dead who
litter the streets like empty bottles
Blood prints on gray pavements
To those who say my voice is too loud—
I say it is not loud enough.
It can *never* be loud enough.

Overpowering? Too Tall?
Well sweetie, I ain't no pushover.

I stand the size of some Trees.
Especially in heels, hair and attitude.
"Call me a Glamazon," says RuPaul,
and she speaks the truth.
If I am overpowering,
then let me use my abilities well.

Let me overpower you with
Knowledge, Magic, Justice.
Kindness, Righteousness and Hope.
Let my height cast not shadows
of fear and intimidation
but flickering triangles of
diversity and affirmation.
A recognition of linkages and
commonalities,
as well as an honoring of difference.
Am I really overpowering you?
Or is it fear
overpowering
yourself?

And to those who say I am too angry,
I would remind you that I am not angry for
anger's sake.
I am outraged and indignant,
pissed off about
injustice, abuse, hatred and self-hatred.
You know, oppressed people are supposed to
always be kind, accessible, non-threatening,
obsequious, fawning, reassuring, not overly bright.
In sum, we are supposed to know our place.
Well, the place that you allot me sure as
hell ain't big enough!
And the limited feelings you
allow me aren't vast enough.

My goals, just like yours, are simple—
not only to survive
but to thrive, live well and prosper.
But most important to me is to
enGENDER change
Wherever I go.
And I will use
My voice
My height
My anger, and above all else,
My power.
I hope that you use yours too,
not to oppress or demean but to
uplift and cherish.

We all have our own
power poems to write.

So tell me:
what is
yours?

I'm Doin' It My Way

A tired lyrical refrain
From "Old Blue Eyes"
takes on a vibrant new life, I think,
when radically re-applied.

Every day I struggle to imprint my
visionary stamp.
Often I am in opaque darkness,
blind and childish,
reaching through interminable stretches
of exhilarating night.

Screeching at lunar glows
Blind-sided by overpowering
sunshines
Demanding to be seen, heard,
comprehended.

Who the hell am I to think
I can bend the whole world to my liking?
One old soul battling against the
tides of enmity
Swelling with sour rages
embroiled in salty bitterness
But how many before me have had
the same deliberation?
and how many after me,
ponder the same hope-filled musing?

Let's put clichés aside.
let's forget preciousness
and cynicism
for a hot minute.

Despite untold stretches of horrors,
anxieties, and personal terror,

I am trying to grow my fingernails
into machetes.
There is no pre-existing path for me.
I am attempting, often in vain,
to clear the way to freedom,
to slice through to justice,
to sear my own memory
with that slippery thing called
Love.

It is a path with omnipresent thorns,
sinking into tender flesh,
releasing droplets of
crimson all over my ivory skin.

Slashing brush along highways of
convention and conformity
My cheeks burn with the glow
of anguish and fear

But, deep inside,
I can't let the pitfalls stop me.
Some naïve, infantile belief makes me keep
going.
The joy of trying, attempting, forging,
the brow-sweat of release,
streaming sweet liberation.
Even if only rhetoric saves,
I will take the pill,
and so you must.

To comrades in slashing I declare:
onward in the beating sun
Forward in the moon-filled nights.
The path is long, torturous and above all unsure.
But better to try, integrity intact,
than jump into a lake of demonic temptations.
Overflowing with the knowledge

that change is in the air—that it is the beads of
sweat glimmering on your weary brow.
As sister Audre Lorde said:
We were never meant to survive
but inciting a single profound change
is more than they meant us to have.

So the path is long, torturous, and above all unsure.
But damn-it it is righteous
And we are going to make it
And we are going to clear a wide walkway
for those who retrace our footsteps,
when we are eagerly watching from the
other side of eternity.

"S/he did and lived it hir* way."

Joelle Ruby Ryan's planned epigraph

* "S/he" and "hir" are alternative gender pronouns

Smiling

One day I see an old man approach me
He tells me to smile
I quickly oblige him and walk away.

It is only days later that fires erupt
At the base of my spine and start blazing.

You: 80-something, straight,
white man from NH.
I hope I have the privilege
of living as long as you do.

Two Black Trans Girls were recently found
in our lovely nation's capital
their bodies riddled with bullets
shot execution style.
Age? 18 years old.

Sorry if I don't feel
like smiling today.

Some women in the trans community
are considered "mothers" by the age of
24
for to survive that long is considered
old age.

I do not know the story of the old man
who told me to smile.
I'm sure he has faced his share
of hardships, too.
But I do know this:
Smiling cannot be compelled,
cajoled, ordered or demanded.
It is a spontaneous affair
Like a wink,

or a hiccup,
or a tear.

I smile in the arms of a Sister,
Or on the phone with a friend
who waxes ironic.

I smile at the sweet-smelling lilacs
blooming outside
or at the exuberance of
untamable ocean waves.

My friend's father recently passed away
A strong Union man with a gentle spirit,
he'd take a stranger in off the streets.
But his advice on smiling was this:
"If someone tells you to smile, you tell them to fuck off."

Amen, Brother. Amen.

Campus Contradictions

A Chicana Lesbian Feminist
Performs
Live on stage
Fiery and passionate
Exploding healing words
Thriving passion
Hurling out truth and compassion
Cajoling care in an era of
Indifference
Pushing queer power
Into an assembled huddle
Eradicating fear
One less obstacle to
Loving community.

Leaving the temporary oasis,
alone
I am thrown to the
amorphous masses.
Pushed off the sidewalk again
A gang of frat pigs
Reeking of Polo and Tommy
Starched white shirts and
colored dangling
Phalluses
Masculinist cavorting
Laughing at the Amazonian
Gender freak.

But who will have the proverbial
last laugh?

I see you dangling from your
cherished neck ties
Clean-cut, straight, white boys
In pressed white shirts

Caught in their own macho
Noose.
Swaying with outstretched tongues
My own queer fingers
Crimson-painted fairy nails
Tightening the gender
Knot.

Purpose

I stand alone
Staring out at the vastness
Of this crazy place we call
Earth.

My head splitting apart from a
Frenetic pace
My body twitching and unsettled
From too much caffeine and sugar
Orifices ready to expel toxicity.
People endlessly rushing past me,
through me, into me
All with someplace important to go
Something important to do.

In the whirlwind of their/our own making,
I plant my large feet onto the mud
And try to feel connected to
Mother Earth.
As bullets whiz past my head,
I feel only the cool, marshy mud
The earth's fleshy body
Against my feet.
Internally I feel one thing
and one thing only,
for the first time in many moons:
Purpose.
My Purpose, right now:
To survive
To live
To thrive.

Fuck:
the deadlines.
The self doubt
The hatred

The nay-sayers
The bigots
The lethal dose
poised at my veins.
Fuck it all.

My purpose:
To survive
To live
To thrive
To feel the love emanate from that
soft squashy mud
throughout my body
for all of my days.

Purpose.

To Be Real

Walking down Main Street USA
Blur of black,
Vertical six-and-a-half-feet
Gender Unknown.
Step, walk. Walk, step.
Passing by and looking away.

How to explain to the
normals of the world
I do NOT exist
To make you feel real.

To be real
Is not to be
In opposition
To any living being
On this planet.

To be real is not a negative entity,
it is passionately
Positive.

It does not detach,
detract, or
denigrate.

Do you see yourself
through my own inverted
Reflection?

Do you create your own image
through rendering me un-seeable?
Are you visible because I am
invisible?

How vexing
Unseemly and
Alien
To be looked at,
but not seen.

When I speak out my voice,
scream out my anguish
Whisper my desire
Do you ever hear me?

Walking down Main Street USA
There is nary a moment I feel completely
at ease
Perhaps my relation to you
has been learned
All too well.

When you throw change at me
Glare at me
Spit at me
Curse and rail against me
I come to expect it.
When a smiling passerby
looks into my eyes
I am momentarily shocked
Brought back to the stillness of
this
lucid moment.
The solid tar of the pavement
Heavy under my feet.

To be real is
positive presence
It is emotive excess
In the eyes of a stranger
I become concretized
Baptized in the ocular act of

Consumption.
It is fleeting,
of course.
But isn't it always?

Anyways, it is enough
for now.

This lesson and
this prayer
for all of
us.

To Be Real.

What's in a Name?

I.
My document pops up on
MS WORD 97
On my dad's new Gateway
Electronic cursor flashing and blinking
I start editing and clicking away
But notice something in the corner
"J-O" has undergone a ghostly
transformation to
"J-O-E"
You see, daddy doesn't like "J-O"
He likes "J-O-E"
I move the cursor to the right of
"E"
and hit backspace.
The "E" speedily disappears.

Sorry, daddy.

II.
On a sweltering August afternoon
I makes my way into the courtroom
for some "Official business"
A legal father peers down at me
from the bench
I am in silk orange Capri's and a blouse
Long flowing scarf, insouciant as can be
Until …. The INQUISITION begins:
How long have you been doing this?
Are you in therapy?
Are you on hormones?
Are you getting the operation?
Why do you want to do this?
Where do you work?
Do people know about you?
What about dating?

Beads of sweat start pouring down
from my forehead
Streaming against my pancake makeup
I try to stand clam and unswerving.
"Yes, sir."
"No, sir."
Thinking bowing down
to the patriarch with a J.D.
will get me my coveted piece of paper
Declaring the birth of "Joelle."

III.
Eager, heart pounding trips to the mailbox
through the autumn.
Where is the promised "written ruling?"
It takes forever and I have to call
The woman states it takes longer with
adoption cases and
trans…….
Mmmmmmm
 transssss…….
Transsexuals you mean?
Yes.
That'd be me.

Finally the letter arrives.
Official typewriter print on
white envelope to Mr. Joseph N. Ryan
I rip it open, mangling it in the process.

"That he considers himself (sic) 'transgender' is
considered inadequate to meet his burden
when balanced against the countervailing
dangers of deception and confusion to the
public. The petition is [bold letters]
dismissed."

IV.
My blood father denies me my identity.
"J-O" becomes "J-O-E."
My legal father denies me my identity.
"Joelle" reverts to "Joseph."
I do not exist on this planet to
please, placate, entertain,
solidify or strengthen
YOUR identities, Father.
I exist to create, transform,
explore and revolutionize my own.
And ain't neither one of you
Daddies
Going to ever halt
My Journey to
Freedom.

Do You Have a Wee-Wee?

I.
walking in Market Square
Portsmouth, NH
you intrude into my reality
making kissy-kissy noises
you ask if I want to go for a ride
or if I would date you
my companion Melina is
spooked by you
and wisely wants to walk in the
opposite direction
but I persist, refusing to walk away
and then, the piece de la resistance,
"Do you have a cock?" you scream out
you are young, white, macho male
full of bravado and hatred
"Excuse me?"
"A cock. A wee-wee."
you actually said wee-wee,
reverting back to immature boyhood
I feel like this is yet another
peeing contest
My middle finger instantly pops up
"Fuck you! Fuck you! Fuck you!"
I yell in rage.
then you peel off into the distance.

II.
Over maki rolls,
Melina attempts to instruct me on
proper chopstick usage, but I cannot
concentrate on my lesson.
Only on this young bigot,
teetering on the brink of manhood.
Even the wasabi burning my nasal

membranes does not allow me to forget
his sneering face.

He was trying to
figure out
whether
to fuck me,
or kill me,
or perhaps both.

I do not maintain any
illusions about America.
I am not a patriot or
flag-waving champion of America.
More often than not,
I despise this country of hate and lies.
I mourn for my dead sisters every day,
and the many deaths that we are
assaulted with each and every day.

But how to not to take the bait—
and further
the very bitterness
that he spit into my mouth?

I have no facile answers,
only a continuing
devotion to justice and freedom,
and a desire to end young punks'
domination and bigotry.

To Melina: I am sorry I didn't run away,
but they keep chasing me and catching me
and I all I want to do now is fight back.

I have never been in a fist fight in my life.
Despite numerous attempts on my life.
But never was I so close to bursting my foot

through the car window,
to ramming a fist down his throat.

The rage boiling inside of me
will not simmer down,
and frankly,
I don't want it to.

To the young man who asked
"Do you have a cock?"
I offer a question to your question:

"Why the fuck do you want to know?"

VI.
Just Say "No!" to Assimilation: Forwarding Radical Resistances

United We Stand

The Queer Community is not
a cargo plane.
We cannot jettison those deemed
"unacceptable"
in the hopes of a safer, lighter passage.

We humans are not expendable packages.
We cannot survive being thrown
like raw meat to sharp-toothed sharks.

Trans, Gender Variant, Drag and Intersex
Have always been a part of this movement.
Those who say otherwise ignore
vital realities of our shared histories.

On a sweltering June night in 1969
a trans queer threw the brick that
ignited a Revolution.
Those unnamed warriors risked so much,
and received far too little in return.

Today, over 30 years later, the
assimilationist-minded
gay men and lesbians rule supreme.
Trouncing all over the gender queers
in an act of supreme arrogance and
acute loss of memory.
They are forgetting so much and
losing far too many.

At this time of static dread,
or worse active regression,
we must quickly and loudly
sound the proverbial alarm.
We are all different, and yet the
blood shed

proves we are all the same.
If we do not stand together,
fight together and join hands in battle,
you can be sure as hell we will not survive.

This does not mean collapsing differences,
minimizing uniqueness,
or quelling disagreements.
It surely means a renewed vigor
and attentiveness to these very issues.
But we must reach a groundswell of consensus
as bigots continue to yank away our hard-won rights.

Fear drives a divisive wedge
but we must not allow it to accelerate
our own destruction.

Butch Dykes, Flaming Queens, Nelly Boys,
Drag Kings, Trannies, Herms With Attitude,
Gender Variants, Dykes on Bikes, Bi-Genders,
Multi-Genders, TransFags and BoiDykes…
The list goes on.

Look at the spectrum of gender diversity.
A Goddess-given strength to our
Movement.
Be Fierce
Be Flamboyant
Flame trails for yourselves and
your fellow queer warriors.
Stand tall in stilettos
Teetering on the brink
Wishing for nothing less than a
Gender Revolution!

Do Not Pass

on the bus, heading towards Amherst, MA.
en route to another academic conference
I keep seeing the same sign:
DO NOT PASS
a not-so-subtle irony to me,
a transgender warrior who battles every day,
to be visible, truly seen,
listened to and understood as what I am-
not a woman, not a man, but an uppity tranny,
6'6" tall, size 14 woman's shoe,
the face of an androgyne,
hands with fingers that stretch skyward.
chest flat as an Iowa cornfield,
it's easy for most to tell what I am:
a girly boy, a she-male, a shim—
they call me many names.
but those signs which I keep seeing
everywhere are a powerful reminder
DO NOT PASS
do not hide, do not conceal, do not front,
do not live in shadows or closets, secrets of shame
take off the masks and step out into the startling dawn
see the world as you've never seen it before
there are so many masks to remove

to People of Color
be proud of your racial and ethnic background
speak boldly and proudly about your heritage
do not buy into the "White is right" garbage
as a white person I can definitely tell you that
we don't know what the hell we are talking about!
our "superiority" is a lie which keeps living on
bi- and multi-racial people: learn to love mixture,
ambiguity and hybridity
a melding of culture

you stand as the blueprint of a new world
step out loudly into the morning and give 'em hell
DO NOT PASS

to the poor and working class,
to people on welfare, SSI or food stamps,
to first generation students and scholars
to blue collar warriors the world over
politicize your status,
talk about it to anyone who will listen
be proud of your working-class roots
and proud of the work that you do
work for change, unionize and study Marxism
do not kowtow to management,
the elite few, the corridors of capitalistic
power and excess
do not allow shame or guilt
to seep into you because
you can't keep up with the joneses
fuck the joneses!!!
Work to squash the myth of the amerikan dream
Call the rich and privileged on their entitled bullshit
do not pretend to be a member of the
middle-class if you are barely scraping by
from month to month
DO NOT PASS

Women of the world—be loud, walk tall,
be proud of what you look like and
how much you weigh
Do not submit to anyone, especially macho pigs
Do not acquiesce to the patriarchal system
Rebel, resist, raise your fist and
demand an end to sexual violence,
intimate partner abuse and harassment
Demand equal pay for the work you do
and acknowledgement for the work of
rearing children

Do not be afraid of the "f" word: feminism
Raise your daughters to respect themselves and
to fight for what they believe in
Be radical and uppity and bitchy.
Be snippy and snappy and brassy
and subversive. BUT
DO NOT PASS.

Queers of the world
Burn down, tear down and rip open that closet door.
Once and for all and forever!
Be out always, everywhere, and to everyone.
You have absolutely nothing to be ashamed of!
Be butch, be femme, be androgynous,
Or none of the above
be flamboyant, be fierce.
Shake that ass on the queer dance floor of life.
Snap those fingers and be queer as fuck.
But please!
DO NOT PASS

Imagine a world where nobody passed
But instead spoke their truths
Lived their unique realities
Took off the masks
And stopped fronting and perpetrating a fraud,
To emulate the people in power.
You may not fit into any of the above categories,
but that's okay.
I know everyone is passing somehow
So, people of the world, the next time
you see one of those innocuous street signs,
think about what it really means
About what the planet would look like
if we all took those simple three words to heart:
DO NOT PASS.

Why MTV Sucks

Channel surfing one day,
I notice that MTV has a new campaign:
"Fight for your rights.
Take a stand against discrimination."
I laugh bitterly and ponder the irony.
MTV: discriminator, par excellence,
and a company which absolutely exemplifies
corporate malice and hypocrisy.

This is the same corporation which,
while decrying Matthew Shepherd's death,
makes a cheap, insulting
movie-of-the-week about his life.
Then parades Eminem on stage,
grants him awards and lauds him as a genius.
This, despite the fact that his favorite word is
"faggot"
and he calls for the murder of his own
wife and mother, and by extension,
all women.

Par for the course for a channel which spins
countless booty-shakin' rap videos which
present Black Women as "bitches" and "hoes"
and Black Men as thugged out pimps who
care for nothing but partying and making G's.
Well, let me tell you:
It AIN'T all about the benjamins,
for Black People or anyone else.
But apparently for a corporate giant like MTV,
that is precisely what it is all about.

Radical black liberationism, feminism,
genuine queer and trans empowerment and
socialism cannot pay the bills at MTV,
so you don't see it on their twisted channel.

To MTV I say:
Don't insult those of us struggling to survive
at the margins with your
pseudo-political, hypocritical,
booty-shakin', money-makin',
queer hating, gender baiting,
Black People downing, white male CEO crowning,
boy band showing, no where-going,
Brittney Spears singing, silicone breast slinging,
saccharine pop ringing, status quo clinging,
"Alterna" band faking, shameless money raking,
free-thinking closing, body-fascism imposing,
Eminem and misogyny lovin',
capitalist, patriarchal shovin',
endless stereotype displayin',
revolutionary delayin.'

I have had enough!

Yeah, you got some eye candy
to zone me out from time to time.
But what is the substance behind the lights,
glitz, commercials and cheap talk?
For all these reasons and more:

MTV Sucks!

Porno Spam

N'Sync caught on tape naked
Jennifer Lopez butt-fucked
Christina Aguillera sucking cock
Horny housewives
Free, nasty, live, teen sex shows
Boys and dogs, girls and dogs
Nasty dogfart sluts taking it hard
Restrained, abused, beaten and used
Young snobby chicks getting hammered
Sickest bitches ever
Abused little girls crying
Girl raped by mad donkey
Cum sucking hoes
Incest Incest Incest
Fresh rape web site
Cum dribblers
Cum swallowers
Cum facials
Free animal sex
Welcome to brutal rape action
Watch me suck dick live
Cum watch me screw for free
Global rape archives found
Mega collection of brutal rapes
Easy, sleazy beautiful cover girls
1,000,000 Free XXX Pix

Sex is used as hate speech every single day
We're told we have free speech
but really we have no say.

Girls and women horrifically abused
Slapped, and raped
and psychically bruised.

Sex sold to make money is about
power and dominance
Misogyny and sexism is what
really shows prominence.

Who profits from this and
who suffers pain?
Who fills their pockets
while others are slain and go insane?
The erotic is power and
can do much valuable work
But it can't be commodified
by some blood-sucking jerk.

Now I am not anti-porn, a prude
or a hypocrite about sex
I just think it's a topic which is crucial,
far-reaching and infinitely complex.

For when I open my email
and these are the words littering my in-box
I know that sex as we learn about it is a
mysterious paradox.

Taught to never discuss it and
always hold our deepest passions in
Then these words and images parade
that forbidden fruit as dirty sin.

If little girls abused and crying is
marketed as a turn-on
And rape and bestiality are "sexy"
then society is truly far-gone

When I think of the tears of people
sexually abused in this nation
The incest, the rape, and the never-ending
exploitation

Then I know that this porno spam
is not simply benign
And it's time for our country to look at sex
and radically redesign.

To reclaim the erotic as a source of
strength and power
Where no one is degraded or
forced to fearfully cower.

Sexuality could be empowering
and as free as a dove
To repeat a well-know question:
Where, oh where, is the love?

A Poem to Gay Sell-Outs

One decade ago
Raised, clenched fist
What about the goddamn "T" ?
Why are we never included?
I don't want to drown in your alphabet soup.
I demand recognition, validation,
own up to Stonewall!
Sylvia Rivera and Marsha P. Johnson.
Trans Gender Queer Warriors
Who paved the way
The tranny choir kept getting louder
Until GLB became GLBT
And we thought we were winning the battle,
taking back our legacy.
Reclaiming the spirit of radical rebellion
Us gender queers have been here a long time
But a letter is a letter
And let me tell you, girlfriends
It ain't made shit happen for trannies

Sorry I'm not a toned, nautilized, waxed, butch,
tanned, buzz-cutted, goateed fag with
Versace jeans and tank top
Or androgynous, middle-of –the road,
corporate, rainbow-flag-waving, pseudo-feminist,
HRC, Elizabeth-Birch wannabe power dyke

I AM
Queer as gender fuck
Polymorphously perverse
Unsmiling tree-tall Amazonian
Transfeminist uppity wo/man,
who is sick of assimilationism,
conformity and a lack of gall and guts.

It is time for revolution,

and as always, it's gonna take everybody
whose fierce and unafraid.
If the system's tailor-made suit fits you fine:
wear it and get lost.
If you have a problem with cross-dressers,
trannies, hermaphrodykes, transfags, boi-dykes
and the like:
You can kiss my princess ass!
You bourgeois guppy reactionary.
Go mingle with the Log Cabiners and vote for
Dubya again!

Because GLBT is a broken promise
Ten years ago I started off fresh, eager,
hopeful and invigorated
Now I'm jaded, cynical.
The mirror cracked a thousand fold
and refuses to be reconstructed

As we speak, those bourgeois gays are trying to
write my people out of history.
Remove us from community centers.
Throw us out of "womyn-born-womyn" only spaces.
Excise us from legislation meant to protect and empower.
Sacrifice the gender queers on the alter of conformity
and let the fringe fend for themselves.
With friends like these, who needs enemies?

Is it time for trans separatism?
A movement solely for radical trans comrades?
No sell-out gays, lesbians allowed.
Try that on for size. And tell me how YOU like it.

The question no longer is:
are you gonna let us jump aboard the truck?
The question is: are we gonna run over your ass?
En route to radical unstoppable unswerving
gender freedom, gender justice and gender liberation.

If you wanna ride, stick out your thumb honey.
I might just decide to forget history and pick you up.
But be quick.
Gender queers ride at
lightning speed.

Gender Suspects

STOP!!! Gender Suspect # 1.
Finger-snapping, Glamorous
Sashaying Queen.
Glittering Tiara on teased-up
Tresses.
Teetering on spike heels,
Lee Press-ons vehemently Red
Reading and throwing shade
Fierce as a motherfucker
Thrown into a paddy wagon like so much
Gender trash.

STOP!!! Gender Suspect # 2.
Black leather jacket wearing
Dyke.
Clean-as-snow white tank top
Tight blue jeans pulled over
full, womanly hips.
Breasts ace-bandaged down
Hair shaved down to the bone
Classic butch swagger in
shit-kicking Doc Martins
Handcuffed by the men in blue.
Another gender casualty.

STOP!!! Gender Suspect # 3.
Me.
Caked-on Max Factor pan-stick in
Nude Ivory
Piercing purple gothic lips
Glamazon height
Draped in Midnight black
Eternal twilight velvet
A night-time androgyne
Neither here nor there
Unknown and uncharted

nether regions
Chained in spite
To the other gender rejects.

We Stand
Gender Suspects # 1, 2, and 3
Gazed at in the police lineup
Our fear disguised by pride
Fogging up the one way glass of their
Ocular consumption
Cuz Houdini ain't got nothing on us
Broken free of a sadist's shackles
Nails sharpened to blades
Spike heels transformed into deadly weapons
Bad-ass leather belts looped into a noose
Shattering their gender mirror
Into countless fragments
Rampaging against the blue menace
The rage of countless abused gender warriors
guiding our bold steps outward
the gender cops startled at their own ineptitude
to contain us and stop us
the bitter tears of our arrested queer ancestors
guiding our brazen steps toward freedom.

Suspects
No More.

G to the L to the B to the T

G to the L to the B to the T
We're one big queer family,
can't you see?
G to the L to the B to the T
Stands for unity and equality
Or so they keep telling me
We're one big queer family,
can't you see?

But it seems to me that we ain't all free
Some L's and G's don't seem
too fond of B's and T's
They think that in order to create a
better society
We need to hold back on B and T
Because it's G and L that are the key
They say the struggle is all about
homosexuality
And those B's and T's, they just need to
get down on bended knee.
Well, Honey.
I got a message for all you
sell-out L's and G's
It's time to put you in a deep freeze
I flatly refuse to be
Your unsightly discarded gender sleaze
Because might I remind you that the
big queer tree has many leaves
Myriad colors ALL—from pink to lavender
to orange to burgundy
Backward L's and G's must stop making
B's and T's pay a fee
We've paid our dues and still
maintained our sanity
No matter how hard you

assimilationist L's and G's try,
Us B's and T's ain't gonna flee
We're going to sing and shout and write poetry

Now don't get me wrong, please
I'm not trying to bust up the movement or
create disharmony
I just want you truly to see
That none of us are free, until all of us are free
Cuz we have so much en-er-gy!
We can go on a revolutionary spree
And if we work together,
we might even win victory
But only if G and L remain with B and T,
locked in solidarity
Shoulder-to-shoulder,
pressed in proximity
So let's make like the army
and be all we can be
Grenades turned to lilies and bullets
to flaming pansies
There are so many different queer flowers
All passionately blooming on the same tree

BECAUSE......

G to the L to the B to the T
We're one big queer family,
can't you see?
G to the L to the B to the T
Stands for unity and equality
Or so they keep telling me
We're one big queer family,
can't you see?

Fuck Your Binaries !!!

I am NOT

Gay or Straight

Male or Female

Masculine or Feminine.

I am NOT

Butch or Femme

Top or Bottom

Dominant or Submissive.

I refuse to situate myself in your

Dichotomous World

With all your Black-or-White labels

I am a dangerous Wo/Man:

slippery and ambiguous and impossible to

PIN DOWN.

I revel in difference,

wade into the sea of impossibility waist high,

and feel the cool water of

Freedom caress my flesh.

If the water scares you,

and if you need the shore,

then go bake in the desert sun.

Collude with the notion of Separatist Space:
the illusion of some safety to be found,

the firmness of the land already

shifting under your feet.

I am proud to be an Indecisive Libran,

and my identity can flow like droplets

through your Outstretched Fingers.

Do you need to put me in your boxes?

Do you need to place my Queer/Trans body

Up to the mirror of your own Vision,

to solidify your own entrenched position in the earth?

To you

I am un-seeable,
un-knowable,
un-touchable.

But you cannot crucify me to your

either-or mentality.

I won't be your dimorphous martyr.

Like a multicolored gem I will shine

in the orange sunburst,

Multiple layers of light refracting

through a somber gray world

And I will make a home out of a sea

of radical diversity,

a changeling and a rebel

to the Last

Violet Sunset.

On the Dotted Line

Sign
On the dotted line
Honey, there ain't no fine
Your signature is a lifeline
We'll Thwart all attempts to malign
And Herald the Blessed Androgyne
Weaving an impenetrable vine
Queers and feminists will intertwine
And nobody will manage to outshine
Nor will they undermine
Our impassioned attempts to
Reassign, realign or redesign
the unique imprints
Of the Twilight Gender Divine.

Our pace is frenetic, enduring and energetic
Our gender expressions are sexily aesthetic
Endearingly poetic and sure as hell ain't synthetic!
So a feverish plea to those who are genetic
The time has ended to be just sympathetic
We need to be unapologetic
Fists clenched against the apathetic
Unfurled screams increasingly magnetic

I know we ain't supposed to recruit
but comrades this is a right-on pursuit
Bigots and Sell-outs I will angrily refute
My need and desire endlessly acute
It's time for us to radically reconstitute
Outwit, outlast and even outshoot
I'll offer you my parachute
and gratefully salute
Hatemongers we'll shock and electrocute
but never sink to their level and persecute
It is to *freedom* that we are doggedly en route

So be an ally, a tranfan, a transgender-friender
I promise it won't cause a fender bender
We are a mighty and righteous contender
From the post-op to the cross-dressing weekender
Know that we will Never Ever surrender
Cuz if you're a Gender Defender
you will reap the benefits of
Dazzling Revolutionary Splendor

You see Trannies you just can't confine
Or easily define
We live permanently at the shoreline
Flatly refusing to be society's concubine
Or play the sexual frankenstein
So let me make it crystalline
Sisters and brothers don't you dare decline
Cuz together we can combine
Hearts beating across the bloodline
Invoking the Goddess Spirit of the Serpentine
United we can build a living shrine
Christen it, toast to victory and drink some wine

We'll forge an army at the frontline
We'll thwart all attempts to malign
And herald the Blessed Androgyne
Weaving an impenetrable vine
Queers and feminists will intertwine
And nobody will manage to outshine
Nor will they undermine
Our impassioned attempts to
Reassign, realign or redesign
the unique imprints
Of the Twilight Gender Divine.

Your signature is a lifeline
Honey, there ain't no fine
So I'd say it's High Time to
Sign
On the dotted line.

VII.
Love and Revolution

Feminism Lives

They tell me I'm too opinionated
My views too radical
I shoot people down who don't agree.
They say I'm too angry
Rough around the edges
Too biased, subjective and emotional.

Maybe I am so emotion-filled
Cuz I'm always getting grilled

And I criticize a whole lotta stuff
And to some that may make me seem rough

But here in the United States
My spirit is intertwined with many fates

And I am simply not afraid of rage
In fact I think it can be mighty sage

Generations languish in anger and sadness
Righteous women railing with
vengeance and madness

A lone voice passionately crying out
Or a chorale of warriors who loudly shout

Millions of witches, burned at the stake
Facts covered over and rendered opaque

Healers and midwives stopped dead in their tracks
To make way for gynecologists,
psycho-ologists and quacks

One in three women raped sometime in their life
Wild succulent women forced
to be some man's lowly wife

A woman in the US is beaten every eight seconds
For this fact alone a force in me beckons

Five thousand years of male-supremacist hell
When the glory and splendor of the
Goddess suspiciously fell

Cuz they killed off the people who
worshipped her glory
And concealed and denied to tell us
all HIS-story

Women's herstory covered over with lie after lie
Girls who already hate themselves
and just want to die

Where is the justice in this country of ours?
Freedom replaced with endless chains and bars

George W. Bush doesn't want women to be free
See for him, liberty comes with
an exorbitant fee

Straight white male fat cats living high of the hog
While women and minorities get
swamped down in a bog

Sometimes it all gets me so down I wanna give up
But the Goddess plants a vision in me
that will inevitably erupt

Women may not have won the war
but are winning the battle,
We're sounding the alarm and shaking
a voluminous rattle

United and strong, our shrieks pierce the starry night
Uppity women continuing the legacy of a
dedicated fight

So seize a sister's warm hand
and lend her a compassionate ear
Tell her should-to-shoulder we can make it,
there is nothing to fear

Feel the strengths of the ancestors
guide you on your path
And let the patriarchal pricks
feel your potent wrath

If they look at your words and deeds
and call you a bitch
You look them square in the eyes
and tell 'em you're a feminist witch

Quick-witted, hotheaded and plenty of sass,
With the sinister wisdom
to put a spell on their ass

So if you think I'm too angry
you ain't seen nothing yet,
Blisteringly bold and fervently zealous,
I hold no regret

I'll never be quiet, submissive or meek
For it is a noisy subversion I undyingly seek

So stand steadfastly resolute and
squelch that apathetic yawn
Don't blink!
for you might miss
the dazzling, revolutionary dawn.

Sanctuary

For Bailey

I dreamt about you
Long before my eyes ever met yours.
I did not know what shape,
size or gender you came in.
I did not know the color of your eyes,
the texture of your hair,
the feel of your touch.

I only knew that your body provided
a safe haven,
A sanctuary, a shelter from the continual
onslaught of this
Gender War.

Life for me has proved neither easy,
or simple.
Whether imposed from within or without,
Someone is always chasing me.
Surrounded by hate mongers,
Beat down by bigots,
I looked to the onyx twilight
On many starless nights
My eyes unwavering through
streaming tears
My fists clenched with the
bitterness of 100 martyrs
And wondered aloud whether
I would find the
Strength
To usher in another
orange-burst dawn.

I spoke to the vast black sky:
What is there for me?

Who is there for me?
To fill this unquenchable void
To soothe this gender fatigue
To pour balm over skin roughened
by self-hate
To pluck away the slivers of fear
that dot my body in endless,
orderly rows.

When you appeared
I was startled.
For maybe I had already given up hope
of ever finding you.
I approached every step
With the greatest trepidation
Afraid you would be like all the rest,
and
Leave me in the end
Alone.

But it was your touch that was
Transformative.
Steady, patient and enduring.
Your embrace enveloped me in
velvety warmth
Causing my soul to tingle in ways
that I had never known.
Enraptured, I would get lost in the
kindness of your eyes
Your glance as powerful as a mother tiger tending her
Baby.
Staring into me the kindness
And undiluted love
that the world denied me
or that I denied myself.

In your arms I find peace.
In your eyes I find joy.

As our hearts find a shared rhythm,
and we learn a common language
I feel the glacial sheets
Encasing my spirit start to
Melt—drop by frigid drop,
as you gently pick away at my icicles
and breathe fire
into my deepest recesses.

I dreamt about you
Long before my eyes ever met yours.
And the reality of you:
My prince, my boi, my fellow warrior in the
Flesh
Has surpassed even my dreams.
So now when I feel depleted,
devoid of hope
Not up to the brutal harshness of living
I look to the same vast, black sky
And think of your Gargantuan
Spirit
Enveloping me with
Endless bursts of warmth
Your arms a fortress of Love.

Sanctuary.

Boi Lust

1000 miles apart, I sit
here
yearning for your transformative
touch.

my heart gaining speed as I ponder
the joys of my boi lust
your deep thrust
an insatiable appetite for that charge you
send through my body.

how you—baby boi
enliven in me
a magnetic field of lascivious
possibilities,
bring magnetic spark to a body
that has
lain dormant
for far too long.

a body wracked by fear
insecurity
even hatred—
but along came you:
inciter of lustful pleasure
who is slowly melting away
a sheet of blue ice,
exposing my steamy innards in all their
carnal glory,
emboldening my body in pursuit of
endless cumming.

reveling in gender and
the absence of gender,
our bodies
bizarre to the uninitiated,

unendingly warm and familiar
to each other.

a Towering TransAmazon
And a half-pint tranboi cutey
locked in embrace
savoring the warmth
so seldom found in a
hate-filled world.

cajoling me to heights of
intimacy heretofore unfound
being in your arms makes me stronger,
fuller and
less afraid.

so when I fly home to you boi

know that I am
also coming home to

my

self.

We Didn't Know a Lot of Things

We didn't know a lot of things:
        We fought each other tooth and nail
        Rebuked those who disagreed with us
        Shouted at sisters who didn't think of it our way
        Slighted the woman who dared to do it differently.

We didn't know a lot of things:
        We drank hard and fast and said things we didn't mean
        We passed out in bathrooms, on street corners, in our own
        vomit
        We said "have another" to a girl who already had too much
        We did not steal away the keys from a drunk queen who
        drove away into the black night.

We didn't know a lot of things:
        We gave our bodies to people who did not love us
        We scoured pornography looking for
        one single image of tenderness or love
        we passed over each other in a mad dash for that one "real"
        man or woman who would make us feel whole
        We let others use our bodies unsafely,
        Dreaming that in that one risky embrace,
        We would finally feel loved.

We didn't know a lot of things:
        We let our sister go into court, afraid and alone
        We didn't introduce ourselves to the shy, brand-new tranny
        Sitting quietly and pensively in the corner
        We didn't accompany our friend as she cross-dressed
        And stepped out of the closet for the first time
        We didn't walk back to the car with our girlfriend as she
        teetered
        Out into the deadly night streets.

We didn't know a lot of things:
> We were short with each other: petty and snippy
> And catty and shrill
> We were unkind to each other
> We didn't look out for each other
> And didn't see or acknowledge the myriad ways
> That we were being divided from each other
> By more powerful forces.
> We didn't unite enough in our common struggle.

We didn't know a lot of things:
> We watched sisters cry and did not comfort them
> We watched them lose their home, their family, their
> livelihood
> We watched girls finger the blade of their own destruction
> Play Russian roulette
> Ready the noose
> And did not Act.

Hoping that it would not happen to us.
Thinking we were the "together" ones.
But secretly knowing their fate was always
inextricably bound up in our own.

We didn't know a lot of things.
But we are learning,
Ever so slowly,
to walk each other home.

Gender Quake

It's time for Gender Quake
A radical sex role shake
Ending the great bipolar mistake
The boy/girl divide we will unmake.

Gender Warriors are all over the place
A rainbow of diversity—there is no single face
We fly through the world at a lightning pace
Sparkling our glitter with a steadfast and loving grace.

What we want, of course, is to be completely free
To be full human beings, not your shackled he-she
Life is so short, and sure as hell got no guarantee
To create a new world you must hear our fervent plea.

People are creating change in so many ways
Standing up for who they are, saying this ain't no phase
Liberation is so strong it's truly a craze
So many minds to open, so many trails to blaze.

Gender Quake is not a figure of speech
Transformation has an unstoppable reach
From the majestic mountain top to the pristine beach
We come to organize, rally, preach and teach.

Can you feel the tremors, ripple through the air
The undulating shocks causing righteous repair
It's an earth-shaking affair, oh this I do declare!
A volcano of freedom, for ALL of our welfare.

It will always be tough for us on the fault line
But resistance, my friends, is an encouraging sign
Multiple seismic upheavals will forever realign
A potent desire no malevolent force can undermine.

So, it's high time for a Gender Quake
An end to violence, pain and heartache
Justice, freedom and love will swiftly overtake
Shoulder-to-shoulder, the world we WILL remake.

<u>Afterword</u>

About ten years ago, transgender pioneer Merissa Sherill Lynn looked me in the eyes and said the following: "Always remember that you have more friends than enemies in this world." I was in my early twenties and had only been out as a transwoman for a short period. I thought the saying clichéd and didn't give it a second thought. A decade into this fight, my views have changed 180 degrees. At that time I was young and full of myself, and did not know what was in store for me. Now I see the error of my ways. That saying is literally life-saving. It is easy for those at the top to see everyone as their potential ally; it is hard as hell when you are at the bottom. But believing in people as true allies and friends, even when it seems like you don't have a friend in the world, is a powerful weapon in our own fight for survival and quest for self-fulfillment and community.

Putting these poems out, I feel some fear and trepidation. I know that some will read them and see a lot of bitterness, rage, depression and frustration, and you are correct in this reading. I know that for much of the last ten years I have been beset by sadness and seethed with anger, and while this sometimes has been a positive force to propel me to fight for change, other times I have gotten bogged down in a negative downward spiral. Anger is a double-edged sword. In the words of Audre Lorde, anger used does not destroy, hatred does. I never want my anger, or my righteous indignation at injustice, to turn into hatred. For then I become no better than the oppressor I am trying to stop. Martin Luther King said that unarmed truth and unconditional love will have the final word, and I couldn't agree more. All gender variant people are beautiful because we are trying to speak our own truths and make that known and respected in a world which constantly diminishes our values and tells us that we are sick, depraved, socio-pathic and disgusting. When I think of the love I have received from other gender warriors and allies I get all tingly—for I know that this love is what will sustain us. Love, coupled with justice, are two mighty rivers that no dam can stem and no force of will can halt. It is a mighty current we are fighting against, but in the end I have no doubt that we will win full victory. The gender quake will reverberate for many years to come.

Quite a few years ago I was shopping in a grocery store with my friend Dana in Seattle. A young woman in front of me was buying some beautiful spring flowers. She turned and looked at me and smiled. She took one of the vibrant daisies from the bouquet and handed it to me. She said: I want to give you this flower, because you are a very beautiful person. I thanked her profusely and just glowed with warmth. Earlier that week I had been derided several times on the street, and her words were an absolute balm to my gender-bruised spirit. I held the flower tightly in the palm of my hand and thought: this total stranger had a remarkably positive impact on me. Imagine what friends can do, or families! Each of us have imaginary bouquets filled with thousands of flowers over the course of a lifetime. Either we can greedily horde these sweet-smelling flowers, or we can pass them out to the people we come in contact with.

With this collection of poems, I happily give you some of my flowers. I hope that they inspire you to go out and give away some flowers to people who need them. The difference you can make in their lives is gigantic. This act of kindness by a stranger has been repeated throughout my life. In New York City, a South East Asian man came up to me and said that where he came from, people such as me were honored and cherished. He cajoled me to keep moving forward in this land that is so alien to both of us. A homeless Native American man once picked me out of a crowd of shoppers and put his hands and mine and simply said: May God Bless You. A middle-aged, white woman came up to me after a workshop I conducted and told me that I enlarge the notion of what beautiful is and can be. Transgender allies and youth have come up to me and told me what a positive impact the video *TransAmazon* has had on their lives and on their educational/activist work. An African American feminist at a women's conference talked to me after a transphobic workshop and both provided solace and much-needed wisdom. Nearly every day, in different ways, people from a wide array of social groups have pushed me forward in the work that I do, and for all of their encouragement I am profoundly grateful and privileged.

Recently, I attended a trans conference in New York City. The conference included some speakers from Latin America who discussed the realities of living a transgender life in their respective countries. Maria Bellen Correa talked about the horrific oppression she faced in Argentina from the police and society. As an activist, leader and founder of a group for transpeople, she and her family were targeted for violence and attack, causing her to seek asylum in the US. Even in the face of the state-sanctioned violence, assassinations and cultural bigotry, Maria is more committed than ever to ameliorating society for trans and other gender-variant people in Argentina and abroad. After a workshop, she hugged me and gave me her card in an effort to reach out. After all she has been through, I marvel at her indomitable nature and her spirit of friendship and transnational solidarity. As her colleague Mauro Cabral said emphatically: "We are not victims." The agency of human beings to do transformative work is limitless. As Jess Goldberg, the protagonist of *Stone Butch Blues* remarks, it's not just living through the pain, it's doing something with it afterwards. It's being brave enough to organize to change things. In the past fifteen years, we have witnessed a global explosion to expand gender categorizations and to eradicate discrimination and prejudice against people who break the molds of sex, gender and sexuality. It is these many examples, from all over the world, that must be fuel for our engines to continue the struggle. In a time of imperialism, repression, corporate greed and soaring conservatism, we cannot afford to sputter and become immobilized; our dedication in the coming months and years will perhaps be tested more than ever before.

Through all the negative emotions I have experienced, I still cling to love and its enormous power to transform lives. I guess I am one of those old-school idealists, even in the face of my cynicism. We must not ever let anyone tell us (including ourselves) that we can't leave the world a better place just for having walked on it. In fact, leaving the world in a better position than when we entered it is the greatest and most enduring gift we can ever hope to bestow. May you spread your vibrant flowers far and wide, standing tall in the conviction that will protect and nurture us:

Love and Justice are, always and forever, the only answers. Blessed Be.

About the Author

Joelle Ruby Ryan holds Master of Arts degrees in English and Women's Studies. Currently, she is a doctoral student in American Culture Studies at Bowling Green State University, where her research focuses on gender/sexuality studies and film/media studies. She has taught university classes in English Composition, Women's Studies, American Studies and Ethnic Studies. She is the founder of New Hampshire Transgender Resources for Education and Empowerment (NH TREE) and the co-producer of two autobiographical videos: A Transgender Path and TransAmazon: A Gender Queer Journey. She is a frequent speaker on issues of gender, identity and social justice in classes, community groups and regional and national conferences. She can be reached via the web at www.transpride.org.

CPSIA information can be obtained
at www.ICGtesting.com
Printed in the USA
LVHW030539010721
691577LV00004B/643